the stalin era

1925-1953

by Stuart A. Kallen

Published by Abdo & Daughters, 6535 Cecilia Circle, Edina, Minnesota 55439.

Copyright © 1992 by Abdo Consulting Group, Inc., Pentagon Tower, P.O. Box 36036, Minneapolis, Minnesota 55435. International copyrights reserved in all counties. No part of this book may be reproduced in any form without written permission from the publisher. Printed in the United States.

Photo credits: Archive Photos-11, 14, 47, 55
                 FPG International-24, 31, 38, 41, 51, 57
                 Globe Photos-37, 44
                 UPI/Bettmann-cover, 4, 9, 27

Edited by: Rosemary Wallner

Library of Congress Cataloging-in-Publication Data

Kallen, Stuart A., 1955-
      The Stalin era / written by Stuart A. Kallen ; [edited by Rosemary Wallner].
        p. cm. — (The Rise & fall of the Soviet Union)
      Includes index.
      Summary: Examines events in the Soviet Union during the era of Stalin and his effect on the country.
        ISBN 1-56239-102-X (lib. bdg.)
      1. Soviet Union—History—1925-1953—Juvenile literature. 2. Stalin, Joseph, 1879-1953—Juvenile literature. [1. Soviet Union—History—1925-1953. 2. Stalin, Joseph, 1879-1953.] I. Wallner, Rosemary, 1964-   . II. Title. III. Series: Kallen, Stuart A., 1955- Rise & fall of the Soviet Union.
   DK267.K343 1992
   947.084'2—dc20   92-13474
                                                                                     CIP
                                                                                      AC

table of contents

Page
- 5 the cult of lenin
- 10 a man of steel
- 16 stalin's slaves
- 19 food wars
- 22 harvest of sorrow
- 26 terror in the kremlin
- 34 dividing up the world
- 40 the great patriotic war
- 45 the siege of leningrad
- 48 peace at last
- 49 the curtain falls
- 56 back in the ussr
- 59 from steel to rust
- 61 tears of sadness, tears of joy
- 63 glossary
- 64 index

Lenin's tomb in Moscow.

the cult of lenin

The scientist hurries through the cold dawn breaking across Red Square in Moscow. He enters an imposing tomb and lightly descends the black and red granite stairs. Down into the silent dark he steps, to where the body of Vladimir Lenin has lain since 1935. The scientist opens the crystal coffin, containing the father of Communism, and carefully examines the embalmed corpse. Gingerly, the scientist brushes flecks of dust off the dead man's face. Then, he dabs a special elixir on the waxy skin and returns the glass coffin lid to its proper place.

After the scientist has completed this weekly ritual, he opens a heavily locked door and enters a control center. The only one of its kind in the world, this room's walls are covered with an array of electronic instruments that maintain a steady climate in the tomb. The scientist, whose life's work has been preserving the body of Vladimir Lenin, nods his head in satisfaction.

Whatever political changes may be taking place outside of this tomb, for this week at least, time has not touched the former hero of the Soviet people.

For nearly seventy years, hundreds of scientists from all walks of Soviet medicine and biology have wrestled with the question of how to prevent Lenin's body from decomposing. For it was not only the skin and the bones that were to be kept alive. Lenin's enduring body would also represent the enduring ideals and spirit of the Communist Revolution. The formula that the scientists developed for embalming Lenin has been a state secret for decades. The information has been as jealously guarded as plans for making nuclear weapons. While the bodies of the ancient Egyptian mummies have turned to dust, Lenin is as well-preserved as the day he died.

When Lenin died on January 21, 1924, morticians only hoped to make his body last for six days, until the funeral. It was thirty below zero in Moscow that week. This caused great suffering to the endless thousands of mourners who lined up to pay Lenin their last respects. But the frigid weather also preserved Lenin's body.

After the funeral, fearsome Soviet secret police rounded up dozens of scientists, commanding them to preserve the body of their leader for "two thousand years." The scientists were locked together in a converted street car with beds, washbasins, and a hot plate. There, they labored over the problem at hand. By spring, they had found the formula, and by fall, Lenin's body went on public view.

After his death, a national obsession with Lenin swept across the Soviet Union. The new leaders of the Communist government glorified Lenin in order to manipulate the emotions of the masses and solidify their own power. History was rewritten to cover up many of Lenin's murderous deeds. The city of Petrograd was renamed Leningrad and a proposal was made to rename Sunday "Leninday." Pictures of Lenin's face began to appear on cigarette packs, cups, and even cookies. Within ten years, a Moscow architect had erected a mausoleum. It resembled a cross between the Taj Mahal and the tomb of King Tut.

After his death, Lenin's writings were widely published in dozens of the one hundred languages spoken in the Soviet Union. Reading rooms were set up in small villages so that illiterate peasants could hear the Lenin gospel.

On every army base "Lenin Corners" were set up in recreation rooms. According to detailed government guidelines, Lenin Corners had tables and benches where soldiers could read and play checkers. They also had a staff on hand to answer questions about Lenin, and of course there were drawings and photographs of Lenin and books by and about him. Some Lenin Corners had busts of the man and drawings illustrating events in his life.

In this way, Lenin was elevated to a god-like status to replace the Russian Orthodox religion, which was now illegal. Eventually, every school, library, factory, workshop, and village had their own Lenin Corners. Statues of Lenin were erected in almost every town. Thus in death, Lenin, the man who had outlawed religion in the Soviet Union, became the center of a semi-religious cult that was to last for ten years. He was then replaced by Joseph Stalin, a man who considered himself a living god. A man whose influence would be felt by every man, woman, and child in the Soviet Union.

A statue of Vladimir Lenin in Moscow.

a man of steel

After the revolution that brought Lenin to power, Russia was renamed the Union of Soviet Socialist Republics (USSR or the Soviet Union). The name of the largest Soviet republic was still called Russia. Whatever the name, the Soviet Union at the time of Lenin's death was a defeated country. Between the years of 1914 and 1925, tens of millions of Soviet people had died. Much death and suffering was caused by World War I, the far reaching famine of 1920, and the civil war that had swept all across the Soviet Union. The Communists had solidified their power, but their country was in ruins.

When Lenin died, the pallbearers who carried his coffin were six members of the Soviet Union's governing Central Committee. None of these men realized at the time that Lenin had left a last testament. In this, Lenin gave his views on the ability of these men to succeed him as the General Secretary. Lenin had no good words for any of them.

Leon Trotsky was a bold leader who inspired the masses and was Stalin's friend.

And while he criticized all the members of the Central Committee, his harshest words were for Joseph Stalin.

"Stalin is too rude," Lenin wrote. "I recommend to my comrades that they remove Stalin from his post and appoint it to someone more patient, more loyal, more polite, and more intelligent." Stalin offered to resign, but the other members of the Central Committee rejected the idea. Those men should have taken Lenin's advice. One by one, they were all shot dead, murdered by men carrying out Stalin's vicious orders. The only one who was not shot was Lenin's friend, Leon Trotsky. He was killed by an ice pick through the forehead while hiding from Stalin's secret police in Mexico.

Stalin was an unlikely man to lead a huge industrial power like the Soviet Union. He was not a fiery speaker or a great thinker like Lenin. He was not a bold leader who inspired the masses like Trotsky. As a matter of fact, the few people who knew Stalin well thought him to be a crude, rude peasant. But during Lenin's four-year illness, Stalin made a point to know everything that was going on. He kept all this information on a series of small cards, earning him the nickname "Comrade Index-Card."

Little is known about Stalin's early life. When he was in power, he had facts of his life erased or changed to make himself look better. We do know that Stalin was born Joseph Dzhugashvili in the Soviet state of Georgia on December 20, 1879. His father was an alcoholic shoemaker who died when Joseph was eleven years old, leaving him to be raised by his mother, a washerwoman. Between the years of 1901 and 1917, Joseph lived the life of a Socialist revolutionary. He adopted the name Stalin, which means "like steel," in 1912. He was arrested five times for revolutionary activities and finally was forced to live in frozen Siberia.

Stalin was a hard working revolutionary whose main task was the "liberation" of bank funds. In other words, armed holdups. The money was used to benefit the Socialist Party. Whenever the Socialist Parties split over doctrine, Stalin always took the most radical path. In the end, this left him a member in the Bolshevik Party that overthrew the government of Russia in 1917. Stalin did not help with the revolution because he was in Siberia at the time. Later, Soviet history was rewritten to include Stalin in the historic coup.

Young Stalin in 1911, prior to the Russian Revolution.

After Lenin's death, Stalin moved in to lead the Soviet Union. For several years, he led with two other men; one man was a Party boss from Moscow and the other from Leningrad. This squeezed Leon Trotsky out of his rightful place as General Secretary. On November 7, 1927, on the tenth anniversary of the Communist Revolution, Trotsky organized a street demonstration to protest Stalin's policies. It was broken up by the secret police. Within a month Trotsky was dragged kicking and screaming from his apartment by the secret police and sent into exile.

Meanwhile, Stalin had decided that the Soviet Union was one hundred years behind the other industrial countries. He said "We must catch up this distance in ten years or we go under." In 1928, Stalin unleashed a second Communist revolution. Cruel and daring, it swept away the lives of millions and transformed the Soviet Union beyond recognition.

stalin's slaves

One of the first things to be thrown out was the idea of equality among people. Stalin gave big perks to loyal party members and had managers run their factories like prison camps. Stalin introduced the first Soviet "Five-Year Plan" that laid down impossible goals of production for heavy industry.

Armies of workers were put into forced labor in order to build huge factories. Women had the added hardship of raising children while working. Living in tents and sharing cots, the workers built the largest metal-working plant in the world, massive tractor plants, and giant hydroelectric dams. The Moscow-Volga Canal was built connecting Moscow to the Volga River. Most of the men and women who dug in the mud and laid the stones for the canal never lived to sail down the engineering miracle they created. The canal was dug by hand by thousands of slaves during four years of deadly labor.

In 1703, thousands of workers had died building the city of St. Petersburg for Peter the Great. In the same way, the Moscow-Volga Canal was also a monument to the cruelty of Soviet leaders. This was just one of the massive projects forced into life by Joseph Stalin.

Factory directors competed to meet Stalin's impossible goals, or even to go beyond them. They hijacked trucks and ambushed freight trains to get their hands on sparse supplies. This was theft, but it was better than being thrown in jail or even shot for failure. When it was obvious that the unrealistic goals of the Five-Year Plan could not be carried out, thousands of engineers and specialists were arrested and imprisoned. Some of these engineers were British or German citizens. All of them were scapegoats thrown to the people in order to explain away the hard times. Some officials were jailed for trumped-up charges of sabotaging food supplies. This was a handy way of explaining the food shortages caused by Stalin's policies. Ironically, the jailings removed the talented scientists and engineers who were needed to accomplish Stalin's goals.

In order to run the factories, deliberate food shortages were created to force the people off of the land and into the towns to work.

In five years, seventeen million people were forced off the land they had been farming for generations. Illiterate, wretched, and hungry, they were pushed around by the new ruling elite who despised them.

Once in the factories, the workers were unable to figure out the complex tasks required for their jobs. Expensive and complicated machinery lay rusting because no one could run it. To keep people from leaving their factory jobs, a system of passports and permits was introduced so that no town dweller could move or travel without police permission.

food wars

Stalin believed that the average peasant had too much control over the Soviet food supply. In order to get the peasants to work harder to grow food, he instituted a policy that would make it easier for the government to control the land. One result of this policy was a legacy of inefficient farming that has kept the Soviet Union hungry to this day. Another result was the death of almost twenty million people.

Before the 1917 Revolution, rich landowners produced more than two-thirds of the grain that went to market. After the Revolution, rich farmers were driven out and their houses burned. Lenin gave the land to the peasants. After that, most grain was produced by peasants who were ordered to turn it over to the government. The peasants were not happy with this system, and they mostly ate whatever they grew. Peasants took care of their own needs while the people in the towns went hungry.

A severe food shortage in 1928 called for emergency measures. Thousands of young town dwellers were sent into the country to demand food from the peasants. These young Communists invaded people's homes and barns looking for hidden sacks of grain. Sometimes the raiders returned home to find that someone had raided their home while they were out raiding others. The peasants resisted the raids and hundreds of Party officials were assassinated. People buried their grain in haystacks or abandoned churches. Some burned it or threw it in the river just to keep it out of government hands. By 1929, even less grain was produced, and food rationing was introduced in towns.

To justify this attack on the peasants, Stalin invented a theory to classify the peasants within Communist doctrine. Peasants were divided into three grades: poor, middle, and kulaks. Poor peasants owned nothing and worked other people's land for wages. That made them friends of the Communist Party. Middle people owned and produced enough for their needs, but no more. Kulaks, the Russian word for "fists," were peasants who grew more than they needed and horded food. The categories were considered a joke, but that did not stop Stalin.

Fiery government documents were written debating whether a kulak was someone who owned two or three cows or a person who hired laborers. There was even a classification for someone who only desired to be a kulak. It seemed that a kulak was anyone whom the government chose to name as one.

Whatever the case, Stalin put his propaganda machine to work making the kulak the new enemy of the Soviet people. Stalin's plan was to take back the land that had been given the peasants in the 1917 Revolution. The people would be forced onto huge collective farms run by the state. On his fiftieth birthday, Stalin decided that the kulaks must be liquidated. "We must smash the kulaks, eliminate them as a class.... We must strike so hard that they will never rise to their feet again," Stalin demanded.

harvest of sorrow

By 1930, workers' brigades roamed the country on a mission of "dekulakization." Their slogan was "Drink, eat — it's all ours." If they found food, they ate it on the spot. If they found drink, they did the same thing. They took the shoes off children's feet and the warm underwear off the bodies of their parents. This system starved the hard workers and rewarded the cruel thieves who could not even run the farms. One man came home and found all his property removed except a kettle and a spoon. He was arrested and sent to a forced labor camp in the far northern forest. Another old man took a picture of his home as he left. He was arrested and shot the same evening. Dekulakization was planned for six million people. Party bosses gladly overfilled their quotas. Stalin later remarked that ten million people had been dekulaked.

    Whole villages were picked up, put on cattle trains, and moved to the middle of the Arctic north. The secret police called their cargo "white coal."

Thousands of people died along the way. Millions ended up in slave labor camps, building huge engineering projects like canals and mines. In one project, one hundred thousand slaves died building a canal that proved to be too shallow for ships to use.

Wild rumors swept the country: women were to become community property; children would all be sent to China; old people would be burned in a special machine; the Antichrist was coming and the end of the world was at hand. During the spring of 1930, fourteen million cows and one-third of all the pigs in the Soviet Union were slaughtered by their owners. This would keep the animals out of government hands. No one planted crops. The worst famine in history descended on the largest country in the world.

People ate mice, ants, earthworms, and tree bark. Old shoes were made into a kind of flour. Dead and dying people lay in the streets as wagons came around every morning to pick up the bodies. Human flesh was sold in markets. As the famine raged, the government continued to export grain to other countries. Food was piled on docks and guarded by police, while peasants starved in its shadows.

Starving Russians ate mice, ants, earthworms,

Potatoes rotted while surrounded by barbed wire and soldiers. Party officials justified this unspeakable horror. One man wrote, "Our great goal was the universal triumph of Communism, and for the sake of that goal, everything is permitted — to lie, to steal, to destroy millions of people."

Meanwhile, Stalin's press corps cranked out magazines and books filled with lies. Glossy propaganda magazines showed photos of happy, well-fed Soviets, cheering at the feet of "Uncle Joe" Stalin. The campaign of propaganda, lies, and disinformation was very effective. People in the rest of the world, and many in larger Soviet cities did not learn of Stalin's abuses for decades. However, he could not hide the truth from his wife. In 1932, she shot herself in the head after leaving a banquet celebrating the fifteenth anniversary of the Communist Revolution. She also left a terrible letter for Stalin full of insults and anger.

Five million Ukrainians and a quarter of the entire Kazakh state perished. Experts estimate that up to twenty million people died because of Stalin's policies. The famine that claimed their lives was entirely man-made. It left Soviet agriculture in ruins. But it left the peasantry terrorized into obedience, and let Stalin free to find new targets.

terror in the kremlin

After Stalin's campaign of terror in the countryside, it was not long before he turned his sights to the political opposition in Moscow. Behind the walls of the ancient Kremlin, where the Communists ran the Soviet Union, trouble was brewing for anyone brave enough to question the murderous policies of Joseph Stalin. In January 1934, the Seventeenth Party Congress met at the Kremlin. While most speeches sang the praises of Stalin, some members of the Party tried to promote Sergei Kirov as a replacement for Stalin as General Secretary. Kirov refused the invitation, but within a year, he was shot in the back of the neck by a mysterious assassin who many believed was doing Stalin's bidding. Kirov was not the only casualty. By the time the congress met again five years later, 1,108 of the 1,966 delegates present had been killed by Stalin.

The old Bolsheviks who had been involved in the Revolution for thirty years had been worried ever since Stalin took over.

Stalin making a campaign speech in Moscow

The people who oversaw the unthinkable cruelty in the countryside had become Party bureaucrats. To them, terror was a normal method of governing. When a two-hundred-page document was circulated calling for the expulsion of Stalin, a new wave of terror was unleashed. This time, the terror was aimed at the heart of the Communist Party.

Stalin pretended that he had nothing to do with the murder of Kirov. In fact, he led the state mourning for the assassinated leader. Towns were renamed after Kirov, and the Soviet Union's best ballet company took his name. Stalin claimed that the murder was the result of a conspiracy among Communist officials. Over the next four years, thousands were charged as "murderers of Kirov," and millions more were killed for the alleged conspiracy. The Terror had begun.

Immediately after the dying Kirov was found, a great wave of arrests swept across the entire country. Anyone who appeared in the files of the secret police was dragged into prisons and death cells. Thousands more were deported to the frozen wastelands of Siberia. Stalin began to change the laws to suit his purposes.

In April 1935, Stalin decreed that the death penalty could be used against children as young as twelve years old. Now Stalin could threaten parents with the death of their children.

Stalin gave even greater powers to the secret police known as the Cheka. They were put in charge of the massive and growing network of labor camps in the Siberian region called the gulag. The political prisoners were used to mine the natural resources in that region. In the Siberian goldfields and Arctic lumber camps, few people exposed to the cold and damp survived more than two years. All over the Soviet empire, sick and starving people staffed mining and logging camps. Prisoners were only allowed food and clothing to match their work output.

In 1937, Stalin unleashed another wave of the Terror. First, he made Nicolai Yezhov the head of the Cheka. Tens of thousands of people were dragged from their homes in the middle of the night, tortured, and delivered to slave labor camps.

Yezhov was blamed for the Terror while Stalin's supporters claimed that he knew nothing about it.

No section of society was immune from the Terror. Every village, every home, and every school felt the cold hand of the Cheka. The beatings, executions, and tortures took place while posters of the smiling Stalin gazed down from every street corner in the Soviet Union. Every day, Yezhov sent Stalin lists containing thousands of names of people who would be killed. Stalin examined every list personally and then signed the mass death warrants.

All across the country, neighbors denounced neighbors if they complained about the government. One fourteen-year-old boy became famous when he turned in his own father. Officials erected statues to the youth and quickly named buildings after him. Unfortunately for the boy, members of his family stabbed him to death. A campaign was started to encourage children to turn in their parents. A nation of friends and families was shattered into millions of terrified individuals.

Certain classes of individuals never had a chance in Stalin's mind. Railway men were spies. Engineers were saboteurs. Historians were terrorists.

Lenin and Stalin on a mural in Moscow.

Anyone who had traveled outside of the country or talked to foreigners was arrested. None of the founding members of the Communist Revolution were left alive. Jewish people and most of the Soviet Union's one hundred other minority groups were persecuted.

The Terror became increasingly surreal as the Cheka began to run out of suspects. Astronomers were shot for taking non-Marxist attitudes about sunspots. Anyone writing about anything remotely critical of the Communist Party was shot. Even the secret policemen turned against each other. The Red Army was purged of seventy percent of its commanders, almost 35,000 men. This left the Soviet Army weak and useless on the eve of World War II. Meanwhile, Stalin's propaganda machine cranked out thousands of posters, books, and magazines showing well-fed, happy, and productive Soviet citizens.

By the end of 1938, over half of the population was documented in the Cheka's files. Out of the 250 million Soviet citizens, over twelve million, or one in twenty, had been arrested. The death toll of Stalin's famines, purges, and Terrors will never be known. Experts say that twenty million dead is a conservative estimate.

But to the great misery of the Soviet people, the dying would not stop now. A new threat from outside of the country continued to squeeze the Soviet people. The never-ending rivers of blood would continue to flow.

dividing up the world

By 1939, Germany's Nazi Party was threatening to take over all of Europe. The Soviet Union was in no position to fight a war with Adolf Hitler's well-trained and well-equipped army. Although Germany and the Soviet Union had been "pouring buckets of filth" over each other for years, Stalin believed it was time to make up. In August, Hitler and Stalin signed a secret Nazi-Soviet Pact. The Germans received valuable oil and grain exports while the Soviets received the promise of advanced German military technology. Both sides promised not to attack each other. Communists all over the world were sent into shock when they found out they were in close alliance with their sworn enemy — German fascists. And the people of several small countries were shocked when they found out that Hitler had given them to Stalin.

Poland was the first to fall under the Nazi-Soviet ax. The Soviet Red Army moved in and killed thousands. On June 14, 1940, the Nazis took over France.

The next day, the Red Army marched into the Baltic republics of Latvia, Lithuania, and Estonia. Again, thousands were arrested, tortured, executed, or shipped off to the gulag. Next to fall were parts of Romania and Moldavia. The Cheka made a list of twenty-nine different categories of persons to be arrested in these countries. They included Trotskyists, Jews, stamp collectors, and people who spoke foreign languages.

Stalin's next target was Finland, on the Soviet Union's western border. But the Finns were not so easy to subdue. In heroic battles in dark and snowy forests, small units of Finns on skis killed thousands of Soviet soldiers before the Finns were finally beaten. But the Soviets had paid a high price for their victory. While 25,000 Finns had died, they had killed over 250,000 Soviet soldiers. This proved that the Red Army had outdated equipment and its leadership had been devastated by Stalin's purges.

In the fighting, 30,000 Soviet soldiers had been taken as prisoners of war. They were terrified to go home. Stalin believed anyone who would allow himself to be taken prisoner was a traitor. When the former prisoners of war returned home, they were greeted with bands and congratulations at the border.

The soldiers marched in a victory parade while citizens applauded them. Then they were marched to a railroad station, put on trains, and hauled away to slave labor camps.

By the summer of 1941, Stalin had all the lands promised him in the Pact. In keeping with his end of the bargain, Stalin supplied Germany with tons of grain, oil, cotton, copper, and other minerals. The Cheka helped Hitler's secret police by handing over people who had escaped from Nazi Germany into Russia. The Germans even built a naval base on Soviet soil. Communists in other countries, especially France, helped the Nazis take over their own country because of orders given from Moscow.

But making deals with a madman like Adolf Hitler proved to be another one of Stalin's mistakes. Hitler had written in his book *Mein Kampf* (My Struggle) that "Nothing will ever prevent me from attacking the Soviet Union." And Hitler had a name for this war he planned to wage — the war of extermination. Every citizen would be killed to make way for German expansion. Stalin refused to believe that his good friend Adolf Hitler would attack the Soviet Union.

German soldiers watched huge fires burning in the Russian campaign.

For months, Soviet spies reported that Hitler's army was gathering on the Soviet border. Stalin ignored the warnings. Indeed, officers were shot for suggesting that an invasion was near. Then on June 22, 1941, three million German soldiers invaded the Soviet Union. It was the largest military assault in history. Stalin awoke to find that the Nazis were blasting their way eastward. He had the bringer of the bad news shot immediately.

In Moscow, people were enjoying a perfect summer day. The streets were filled with shoppers and sightseers. By the time the news broke at noon, the German army was racing eastward in a thousand-mile wall of iron death. Stalin locked himself in his office, and drank glass after glass of vodka. He refused to see anyone. The voice of his Foreign Minister, Molotov, crackled through speakers on every street corner, calling everyone to fight the Nazis. Stalin would not be seen or heard from for twelve days. When the Cheka was forced to flee from the Nazis, they murdered everyone in the prisons before they left. Tens-of-thousands of dead were left for the Nazis to clean up.

the great patriotic war

The conflict known as World War II in the rest of the world is called the Great Patriotic War in the Soviet Union. As the Germans swept through the country at a rate of fifty miles a day, many Soviet citizens found renewed support for their country. But in many places the Germans were greeted warmly. Memories of Stalin's famines and purges during the 1930's were still a raw wound for millions. Now the people thought that they had a chance to strike back at the tyrant in the Kremlin. Many people, like the Ukrainians, had suffered so much during the famine that they looked to the Germans as liberators. They greeted the Nazis with gifts, smiles, and hugs. Some supplied the Nazis with important information about Soviet army positions and troop movements. Communist Party officials were dragged from their homes and beaten by peasants who took back their farmland and animals.

Nazi soldiers question an old Russian woman who found shelter in a shell hole. If they don't like her answers they undoubtedly will kill her.

If the Nazis had treated the Soviets decently, millions might have rallied around the Nazi cause and changed the course of history. But Hitler was a slave to his own madness and hatred. He'd come to the Soviet Union not to liberate, but to exterminate, and that's what he did. During the first year of German occupation, millions of Jews, Communists, and others were executed. The streets of towns and villages were lined with corpses swinging from trees. Entire villages were lined up and shot. The Soviets found that they had traded one kind of tyranny for another. The Nazi atrocities drove most Soviets straight into the arms of Stalin. The Germans converted some Soviets into Nazis. By the end of the war over one million Soviets were fighting on the side of the German army.

By October 1941, the German army was in sight of Moscow and Leningrad. Panic descended as people trying to escape clogged the streets. But soon rain poured from the sky. Troops and machines became mired down in the mud. The Germans prayed for an early frost to harden the ground. Their prayers were answered in November when it began to snow.

The frost came hard and fast and it froze German men and machines. Before December, the temperature had fallen to thirty degrees below zero. Thousands of soldiers froze to death. By November 28, over 750,000 German soldiers had perished, but they had taken over one-quarter of the Soviet Union.

Government officials ordered the Soviets to take apart over 1,300 factories, pack them on trains, and move them to the east to avoid German capture. The officials evacuated ten million Soviets with their factories to Siberia. The workers set up machines in fields and worked on war production, while others built the factory walls around them. People who were late to work were sent to the gulag for eight years. To keep property out of Nazi hands, the Soviets filled in wells, ripped up railroad tracks, and burned buildings. Some public buildings were painstakingly camouflaged to hide their identity from the Nazis. The Red Army, some on horseback, fought back bravely in temperatures approaching thirty-five below zero. To them the winter was tolerable.

Russians worked to keep the plane production high. Their motto was "Everything for the front."

the siege of leningrad

Adolf Hitler had always hated the city of Leningrad. He saw it as the birthplace of Communism and believed it deserved destruction. In September 1941, the Germans threw up a blockade around Leningrad that lasted for three years. Three million people were trapped inside the city. Every citizen was mobilized for its defense. They worked at their jobs during the day and dug trenches at night under German bombardment. Soon there was no food. The Germans cut off electricity. People began to starve. The Soviets began to eat anything — including vaseline and wallpaper glue. Cats and dogs were worth a month's wages on the black market. Once again, people turned into cannibals to stay alive. To maintain everyone's sanity, officials played classical music over thousands of loud speakers on street corners. When there was no music, they played a loud ticking of a clock. The violins played on, over the moans of the dying.

The desperate Soviets built an eighteen mile road of ice on frozen Lake Ladoga on the eastern edge of the city. They brought some food in this way between the German strafing. Many trucks were so overloaded that they simply fell through the ice. Even with this pipeline, in January 1942, 200,000 people starved to death. When spring came, this lifeline for food melted into the lake.

Factory workers kept working in the arms factories even as the buildings were blown away by German bombers. As Leningrad's suffering continued, the Red Army was in full retreat, burning everything. They left nothing but scorched earth for the advancing German army. By the end of the siege of Leningrad, 1.5 million people had died, one million of them from starvation.

The battle of Leningrad.

peace at last

On May 9, 1945, the Nazis were finally defeated by the Americans, British, and Soviets. Most of Europe lay in ruins and more than fifty-five million people had died. Twenty million of the casualties, or almost half, had been in the Soviet Union. In addition, 1,700 Soviet cities and towns, 70,000 villages, and 32,000 factories were completely wiped out. No nation has ever suffered so much in war. Widows and orphans lived in holes dug in the ground. Thousands of Soviet soldiers who the Nazis had captured were considered traitors. They were imprisoned, shot, or shipped to the gulag. Some were blown up while being forced to clear mine fields by walking through them. The war was over but the Stalin nightmare continued for eight more years.

the curtain falls

By the end of 1945, the Soviet people were tired of war. They only wanted to mourn the dead and rebuild their lives. The people looked forward to using the war-time industries for peaceful purposes. They wanted housing, education, food, and hospitals. Great celebrations were held at the war's end, and Americans inside the Soviet Union were greeted warmly by the citizens. Many felt the United States had helped save them from Hitler. People even cheered the American flag outside the U.S. Embassy in Moscow.

Inside the Kremlin, however, Stalin plotted his version of the future. Stalin was now an old man with a tired body and failing eyesight. Powerful as he was, he knew he would not live forever. But Stalin still believed in a world-wide Communist revolution. He wanted the Soviet Union to conquer the world for Communism. He privately told his advisors that "in fifteen or twenty years, we'll have another go at it." Stalin intended to launch World War III.

The first thing Stalin did was close off the Soviet Union as it had never been closed before. His purpose was to keep his people ignorant of the outside world. Then people would only have his version of the "truth." The travel of foreigners, especially Americans and Britains, was strictly supervised. No one was allowed to talk to foreigners. A Soviet citizen could be jailed for giving directions to an American on the street. The language was purged of foreign words — French bread became "city bread." Anyone married to a foreigner was arrested and killed. Soviets who had lived in foreign countries disappeared when they returned home. People in factories had to listen to lectures every day about the evils taking place in the rest of the world. People were sentenced to fifteen years in prison for crimes such as "Praising American Democracy" and "Toadyism to the West."

In February 1945, the leaders of England and the United States (the Allies) met with Stalin in the city of Yalta, on the Black Sea. World War II was still raging in Japan, and the Allies wanted Stalin's help to defeat that country. So the Allies made a deal with Stalin.

The Yalta Conference, 1945. (L-R) Winston Churchill,

Over two million Soviets who were prisoners of war or slave laborers for the Nazis were handed back to Stalin, against their will. Some had fought with the Nazis, some were simply trying to escape Soviet brutality. All of them, men, women, and children, were considered traitors by Stalin. And they were all doomed. Many killed themselves before they could be handed back to the Cheka. The rest were shot on sight or sent to Siberia.

When the German army retreated through Eastern Europe, the Red Army was close behind. The people of Poland, Romania, Hungary, and Bulgaria were soon under Stalin's boot heel. All political groups except the Communists were outlawed. The secret police set up shop and soon these countries in Eastern Europe became "satellites" of the Soviet Union. These countries could only trade with the Soviet Union, and the Red Army set up bases on their soil, where they remained for forty-five years. Eventually, Yugoslavia, Czechoslovakia, and Albania also fell to unwanted Communist governance. The same kind of Stalinist terror and propaganda that held the Soviets in its grip was extended to half of Europe.

The leader of Great Britain, Winston Churchill, said that an "iron curtain" had fallen across Eastern Europe. A war of words and threats began between the Allies and the Soviet Union. This war was called the "Cold War," and it would drag on until 1990.

In 1948, the Cold War threatened to heat up when Stalin decided to test the Allies. The German city of Berlin was occupied by the Allies after World War II. The Soviet Union was given its own section of the city. In the spring, Stalin closed all road and rail links to the German capital. The aim of his "Berlin Blockade" was to get the Allies to abandon the city.

The Allies began an airlift to supply Berlin. Every day, hundreds of American and British airplanes brought in tons of food, fuel, and medicine. By the spring of 1949, Stalin saw he was beaten and ended the blockade. Stalin's blockade was a turning point in history. Realizing his threat to world peace, twelve democratic countries including the United States formed the North Atlantic Treaty Organization (NATO) to oppose Stalin. NATO set up army bases all across Europe. Many remain there to this day.

At the end of World War II, the United States dropped two atomic bombs on Japan. Stalin ordered Soviet scientists to develop a Soviet atomic bomb. Soon, the Soviets had their own nuclear bomb. The world watched in fear as the Allies and the Soviets stockpiled thousands of nuclear weapons. The Cold War, many feared, might end with a bang that would kill everybody.

The rising atom bomb cloud after the bombing of Nagasaki, Japan.

back in the ussr

Back in the Soviet Union life was as harsh as ever. Another famine swept across the Ukraine and more starvation resulted. Life in the cities was not much better. Because of all the housing destroyed in the war, dozens of people lived together in one-room apartments. These were the lucky ones. The rest lived in tents or army barracks. The price of bread tripled and an overnight money reform law wiped out the savings of millions of people. Artists, writers, and musicians became the new enemies of the people. They were rounded up and arrested.

Stalin's seventieth birthday was celebrated in 1949 with extraordinary street parties. The Soviet Union and all the satellite countries erected hundreds of statues of Stalin. Factories worked overtime producing small iron statues for people's homes. Stalin's picture was everywhere. In Moscow, dozens of searchlights illuminated a gigantic portrait of Stalin that hung from a balloon in the sky.

Stalin's 70th birthday was celebrated in 1949 with extraordinary street parties in Moscow.

Millions of people marched in the streets chanting, "Glory to Stalin!" and "Stalin is Peace!"

At a ceremony in the Bolshoi Theater, Stalin basked in the glory with Chinese Communist leader Mao Tse-tung at his side. Within a few years, Mao's Red Army, with Soviet help, would be battling American soldiers in the jungles of Korea. The Korean war killed 35,000 Americans, 250,000 Chinese, and two million Koreans. Stalin hoped that the war would weaken Communist China, but instead it strengthened it.

from steel to rust

As Stalin aged, his mind unraveled. He could not remember the names of his closest advisors, and thought everyone was plotting to kill him. His house had more locks, gates, guards, and dogs than a prison. He had dozens of identical bedrooms, and to confuse assassins, he slept in a different one every night. He thought the air in his house was poisoned, and called in top scientists to analyze it.

Everyone around Stalin fell under suspicion. His butler of twenty years was arrested as a spy. His doctor was thrown in a dungeon and kept in chains. His sisters-in-law, whom he'd known for fifty years, were arrested. Their "crime" was knowing too much about his early life. Stalin's taste for blood remained to the bitter end.

In 1953, Stalin arranged for a massacre unlike any yet seen. The men who had survived the purges of the 1930's had been loyal to Stalin for a generation. They'd lied for him, betrayed their families, and done his dirty work.

Now, Stalin believed that they were out to get him. He was going to purge the Communist party, and at the same time, finish Hitler's work by killing all Jewish people. Stalin framed a few well-known Jews, and that in turn cast guilt on all Jewish people. Soon mass arrests swept across the Soviet Union. Stalin said that Jewish doctors were trying to kill him. Panic swept through the country, with people refusing to take medicine given to them by Jewish doctors.

Then as suddenly as it began, Stalin's purge ground to a halt. In the early morning hours of March 2, 1953, a blood vessel burst in Stalin's brain. Guards found him hours later, sprawled on the carpet, unable to speak or walk. His bleeding brain affected the centers that controlled his breathing. Slowly, day after day, and hour after hour, Stalin suffocated. At the last moment, he opened his eyes. They were filled with rage and hatred. He lifted his left hand and pointed a curse at the whole world. At 9:50 p.m., March 5, 1953, Joseph Stalin died.

tears of sadness, tears of joy

The death of Stalin was a national tragedy to countless millions of Soviets. Crowds gathered in weeping masses to mourn the death of their leader. In Moscow, people died in the crush of the crowds as they lined up to pay their last respects to Stalin. He had been the Soviet Union's only leader for almost thirty years, and for many, the only leader they had ever known. Many people had been taught to worship Stalin from childhood and they had sung his praises thousands of times. He'd led them to victory in the Great War, and to many it was like losing a father.

Inmates in the gulag were working when all the lights went out. They sat for hours in the dark until loudspeakers announced, "Our father is dead." Then the inmates cried, too. But their tears were tears of joy. They knew the real Stalin. One slave deep in a mine shaft smiled and said, "I have been here for nineteen years, and this is the first good news I've heard!"

Stalin's mummified body was placed next to Lenin's in the tomb in Red Square. Several years after his death, the new Soviet leader, Nikita Khrushchev stunned the Soviet Union when he revealed the catalog of Stalin's crimes against humanity. Slowly, "de-Stalinization" discredited Stalin and his policies. In 1961, Stalin's body was removed from Red Square. The coffin was placed in a pit filled with tons of cement. A stone slab was placed over the pit with the simple inscription "J. V. Stalin." His reburial began a campaign to remove his portraits from public buildings. Soviets melted down his statues. Cities, towns, factories, streets, and parks bearing his name were given new names.

But the memory of Stalin could not be so easily erased. The secret police, renamed the KGB, still ran the country. The torture chambers, gulags, and prisons still remained. For more than thirty years after his death, the policies of Stalin continued to grip the Soviet Union.

glossary

cannibal — A person who eats human flesh.

Cheka — The secret police force in the Soviet Union from 1917 until 1954. Then, the Cheka became known as the KGB. In the Russian language, Cheka stands for the "Extraordinary Commission to Combat Counter-Revolution and Sabotage."

dekulakization — Terroristic acts performed on Soviet people during Joseph Stalin's rule.

fascists — People who exalt their nation and their race above the individual and who believe in a nation ruled by a dictator. Nazis are fascists.

General Secretary — Title given to the president of the Soviet Union.

gulag — Labor camps in the USSR.

Kremlin — A fortified building in Moscow that contains the government center of the Soviet Union. Also, the name used for the entire Soviet government.

kulak — Peasants who supposedly grew more crops than they needed and hoarded food.

propaganda — The repetition of ideas, information, or rumor in books, newspapers, or the media. Propaganda is repeated with the purpose of helping or hurting an institution, a cause, or a person.

saboteur — A person who disrupts industrial or government goals by means of destruction. A person who blows up power lines or radio stations is a saboteur.

stockpile — A reserve supply of something accumulated within a country.

strafe — To fire at close range with machine guns from low-flying airplanes.

totalitarian — A system of government where all power is held by one person or one group of people.

tyranny — Cruel, evil, and uncaring government or power.

index

Atomic bomb-53,54,55
Bolsheviks-26
Cheka, the-29,32,36,39
Cold War, the-53,54
Dekulakization-22,63
Great Patriotic War, the-40
Hitler, Adolf-34,36,39,42,45,49,60
Iron Curtain-52
Kirov, Sergei-26,28
Kulaks-20,21,63
Lenin, Vladimir-4-7,9,11,12,19,31
Moscow-Volga Canal-16,17
NATO-53
Nazi-Soviet Pact-34
Siege of Leningrad-45,46,47
Stalin, Joseph-8,12,13,14,16,17,19,20-22,25-32,34-
    36,39,40,48-52,56-62
Trotsky, Leon-11,12,15
Yalta-50,57
Yezhov, Nicolai-29,30

13.02

947.084   Kallen, Stuart A.   14347
KAL
         The Stalin era.

$13.02

DATE DUE	BORROWER'S NAME	ROOM NO.
MY 16 '04	Gerard Gonsalves	Savage
FE 23 '96	Jeff Hyde	Taylor

947.084   Kallen, Stuart A.   14347
KAL
         The Stalin era.

GRADY MIDDLE SCHOOL

995873   01302   50630C   00655F